THE POETRY OF BIRDS

Goldfinch *Pablo Picasso*

The
Poetry
of Birds

edited by Samuel Carr

B. T. Batsford Ltd. London

First published 1976
Selection copyright Samuel Carr

ISBN 0 7134 3184 9

Designed by Alan Hamp
Filmset by Keyspools Ltd., Golborne, Lancs
in 12 on 13 pt. Monophoto Bembo
Made and printed in Great Britain by
Butler & Tanner Ltd. Frome
for the Publishers B. T. Batsford Ltd.
4 Fitzhardinge Street, London W1H 0AH

Contents

The Illustrations *6*
Introduction *11*

The Illustrations

The illustrations on the endpapers are from a series of late fourteenth- or early fifteenth-century manuscript drawings in the Pepys Library, Magdalene College, Cambridge.

Introduction

After Love and Flowers, as many poems have been written on the theme of Birds as on any single subject. Fifty years ago H. J. Massingham edited an anthology which, sizeable as it was, left out as many good bird poems as it put in. This small collection aims to include most of the memorable bird poems and to diversify these with some which may be less familiar.

In most poems in this genre the ostensible subject is too often used as a pretext to point a moral or adorn a tale. Here it is the bird itself which is the poems' subject. Good poets are generally people with an exceptional sharpness of vision, and the ability to translate into evocative words whatever it is they have seen. This anthology will succeed if it not only reminds the reader of the birds it describes, but also helps him to look at them with renewed curiosity.

Painters even more than poets see what they depict with revealing clarity. The pictures are intended as a visual counterpart to the verse. They may stimulate and enchant the physical eye in a complementary way to that in which poems work upon the eye of the mind. Few of these pictures are strictly ornithological in the sense that their intention is more to create the actuality of the living bird than merely to reproduce its outward characteristics. A few artists, and Thomas Bewick is certainly one of them, have been both descriptively accurate and creatively true. Jane Eyre, it will be recalled, had occasion to remark, at the very beginning of Charlotte Brontë's novel: 'With Bewick on my knee I was then happy'. It is hoped that the reproductions from *A History of British Birds*, and the other illustrations will similarly please the readers of this book.

Mute swan *Thomas Bewick*

Doves G. B. *Tiepolo*

The creation of birds
from: Paradise Lost, Book VII

Mean while the tepid Caves, and Fens and shoares
Thir Brood as numerous hatch, from the Egg that soon
Bursting with kindly rupture forth disclos'd
Thir callow young, but feathered soon and fledge
They summ'd thir Penns, and soaring th' air sublime
With clang despis'd the ground, under a cloud
In prospect; there the Eagle and the Stork
On Cliffs and Cedar tops thir Eyries build;
Part loosly wing the Region, part more wise
In common, rang'd in figure wedge their way,
Intelligent of seasons, and set forth
Thir Aierie Caravan high over Sea's
Flying, and over Lands with mutual wing
Easing their flight; so stears the prudent Crane
Her annual Voiage, born on Windes; the Aire
Floats, as they pass, fann'd with unnumber'd plumes:
From Branch to Branch the smaller Birds with song
Solac'd the Woods, and spred thir painted wings
Till Ev'n, nor then the solemn Nightingal
Ceas'd warbling, but all night tun'd her soft layes:
Others on Silver Lakes and Rivers Bath'd
Thir downie Brest; the Swan with Arched neck
Between her white wings mantling proudly, Rowes
Her state with Oarie feet: yet oft they quit
The Dank, and rising on stiff Pennons, towre
The mid Aereal Skie: Others on ground
Walk'd firm; the crested Cock whose clarion sounds
The silent hours, and th' other whose gay Traine
Adorns him, colour'd with the Florid hue
Of Rainbows and Starrie Eyes.

JOHN MILTON (1608–1674)

The parrot

A parrot, from the Spanish main,
    Full young and early caged came o'er,
With bright wings to the bleak domain
    Of Mulla's shore.

To spicy groves where he had won
    His plumage of resplendent hue,
His native fruits, and skies, and sun,
    He bade adieu.

For these he changed the smoke of turf,
    A heathery land and misty sky,
And turned on rocks and raging surf
    His golden eye.

But petted in our climate cold,
    He lived and chattered many a day:
Until with age, from green and gold
    His wings grew grey.

At last when blind, and seeming dumb,
    He scolded, laughed, and spoke no more,
A Spanish stranger chanced to come
    To Mulla's shore;

He hailed the bird in Spanish speech,
    The bird in Spanish speech replied;
Flapped round the cage with joyous screech,
    Dropt down, and died.

THOMAS CAMPBELL (1777–1844)

Parrot *Sir Joshua Reynolds*

The Falcon

Fair Princesse of the spacious Air,
That hast vouchsaf'd acquaintance here,
With us are quarter'd below stairs,
That can reach Heav'n with nought but Pray'rs;
Who when our activ'st wings we try,
Advance a foot into the Sky.

Bright Heir t' th' Bird Imperial,
From whose avenging penons fall
Thunder and Lightning twisted Spun;
Brave Cousin-german to the Sun,
That didst forsake thy Throne and Sphere,
To be an humble Pris'ner here;
And for a pirch of her soft hand,
Resign the Royal Woods command.

How often would'st thou shoot Heav'ns Ark,
Then mount thy self into a Lark;
And after our short faint eyes call,
When now a Fly, now nought at all;
Then stoop so swift unto our Sence,
As thou wert sent Intelligence.

RICHARD LOVELACE (1618–1657)

Falcon Jacopo de' Barbari

Birdsong

from: The Merchant of Venice

The crow doth sing as sweetly as the lark
When neither is attended, and I think
The nightingale, if she should sing by day,
When every goose is cackling, would be thought
No better a musician than the wren.

WILLIAM SHAKESPEARE (1564–1616)

Mynah bird and locust tree *Tai Chin*

The blossom

Merry Merry Sparrow,
Under leaves so green,
A happy Blossom
Sees you swift as arrow
Seek your cradle narrow
Near my Bosom.

Pretty Pretty Robin
Under leaves so green,
A happy Blossom
Hears you sobbing, sobbing,
Pretty Pretty Robin
Near my Bosom.

WILLIAM BLAKE (1757–1827)

Sparrow *Thomas Bewick*

On startling some pigeons

A hundred wings are dropt as soft as one,
Now ye are lighted! Pleasing to my sight
The fearful circle of your wandering flight,
Rapid and loud, and drawing homeward soon;
And then, the sober chiding of your tone,
As there ye sit, from your own roofs arraigning
My trespass on your haunts, so boldly done,
Sounds like a solemn and a just complaining:
O happy, happy race! for though there clings
A feeble fear about your timid clan,
Yet are ye blest! with not a thought that brings
Disquietude,—while proud and sorrowing man,
An eagle, weary of his mighty wings,
With anxious inquest fills his mortal span!

CHARLES TENNYSON TURNER (1808–1879)

Pigeons *Carlo Crivelli*

The thrush's nest

Within a thick and spreading hawthorn bush
    That overhung a mole-hill large and round,
I heard from morn to morn a merry thrush
    Sing hymns to sunrise, and I drank the sound
With joy; and, often an intruding guest,
    I watched her secret toils from day to day—
How true she warped the moss to form a nest,
    And modelled it within the wood and clay;
And by and by, like heath-bells gilt with dew,
    There lay her shining eggs, as bright as flowers,
Ink-spotted over shells of greeny blue;
    And there I witnessed, in the sunny hours,
A brood of nature's minstrels chirp and fly,
Glad as that sunshine and the laughing sky.

JOHN CLARE (1793–1864)

Nests *W. H. Hunt*

The blackbird

O blackbird! sing me something well:
  While all the neighbours shoot thee round,
  I keep smooth plats of fruitful ground,
Where thou may'st warble, eat and dwell.

The espaliers and the standards all
  Are thine; the range of lawn and park:
  The unnetted black-hearts ripen dark,
All thine, against the garden wall.

Yet, tho' I spared thee all the spring,
Thy sole delight is, sitting still,
  With that gold dagger of thy bill
To fret the summer jenneting.

A golden bill! the silver tongue,
  Cold February loved, is dry:
  Plenty corrupts the melody
That made thee famous once, when young:

And in the sultry garden-squares,
  Now thy flute-notes are changed to coarse,
  I hear thee not at all, or hoarse
As when a hawker hawks his wares.

Take warning! he that will not sing
  While yon sun prospers in the blue,
  Shall sing for want, ere leaves are new,
Caught in the frozen palms of Spring.

ALFRED LORD TENNYSON (1809–1892)

Blackbird *Thomas Bewick*

A robin

Ghost-grey the fall of night,
    Ice-bound the lane,
Lone in the dying light
    Flits he again;
Lurking where shadows steal,
Perched in his coat of blood,
Man's homestead at his heel,
    Death-still the wood.

Odd restless child; it's dark;
    All wings are flown
But this one wizard's—hark!
    Stone clapped on stone!
Changeling and solitary,
Secret and sharp and small,
Flits he from tree to tree,
    Calling on all.

WALTER DE LA MARE (1873–1956)

The sedge-warbler

In early summer moonlight I have strayed
Down pass and wildway of the wooded hill
With wonder as again the sedge-bird made

His old, old ballad new beside the mill.
And I have stolen closer to the song
That, lispèd low, would swell and change to shrill,

Thick, chattered cheeps that seemed not to belong
Of right to the frail elfin throat that threw
Them on the stream, their waker. There among

The willows I have watched as over flew
A noctule making zigzag round the lone,
Dark elm whose shadow clipt grotesque the new

Green lawn below. On softest breezes blown
From some far brake, the cruising fern-owl's cry
Would stay my steps; a beetle's nearing drone

Would steal upon my sense and pass and die.
There have I heard in that still, solemn hour
The quickened thorn from slaving weeds untie

A prisoned leaf or furlèd bloom, whose dower
Of incense yet burned in the warm June night;
By darkness cozened from his grot to cower

And curve the night long, that shy eremite
The lowly, banded eft would seek his prey;
And thousand worlds my silent world would light
Till broke the babel of the summer day.

RALPH HODGSON (1871–1962)

Cranes *Anonymous Chinese painting*

The kingfisher

from: Upon Appleton House

So when the shadows laid asleep
From underneath these banks do creep,
And on the river as it flows
With ebon shuts begin to close;
The modest Halcyon comes in sight,
Flying betwixt the day and night;
And such an horror calm and dumb,
Admiring Nature does benumb.

The viscous air, wheresoe'er she fly,
Follows and sucks her azure dye;
The jellying stream compacts below,
If it might fix her shadow so;
The stupid fishes hang, as plain
As flies in crystal overta'en;
And men the silent scene assist,
Charm'd with the sapphire-wingèd mist.

ANDREW MARVELL (1621–1678)

Kingfishers *J. J. Audubon*

Ducks *Vittore Pisanello*

The shoot

from: Windsor Forest

See! from the brake the whirring pheasant springs,
And mounts exulting on triumphant wings;
Short in his joy, he feels the fiery wound,
Flutters in blood, and panting beats the ground.
Ah! what avail his glossy, varying dyes,
His purple crest, and scarlet-circled eyes,
The vivid green his shining plumes unfold,
His painted wings, and breast that flames with gold?

With slaughtering guns the unwearied fowler roves,
When frosts have whitened all the naked groves;
Where doves in flocks the leafless trees o'ershade,
And lonely woodcocks haunt the watery glade.
He lifts the tube, and levels with his eye:
Straight a short thunder breaks the frozen sky.
Oft, as in airy rings they skim the heath,
The clamorous lapwings feel the leaden death:
Oft, as the mounting larks their notes prepare,
They fall, and leave their little lives in air.

ALEXANDER POPE (1688–1744)

Parrot and dove

Parrots have richly color'd wings,
Not so the sweetest bird that sings;
Not so the lonely plaintive dove;
In sadder stole she mourns her love,
And every Muse in every tongue
Has heard and prais'd her nightly song.

WALTER SAVAGE LANDOR (1775–1864)

Lady and parrot *Frans van Mieris*

33

Bullfinches *George Edwards*

The Bullfinches

Brother Bulleys, let us sing
From the dawn till evening!—
For we know not that we go not
When to-day's pale pinions fold
Where they be that sang of old.

When I flew to Blackmoor Vale,
Whence the green-gowned faeries hail,
Roosting near them I could hear them
Speak of queenly Nature's ways,
Means, and moods,—well known to fays.

All we creatures, nigh and far
(Said they there), the Mother's are;
Yet she never shows endeavour
To protect her warrings wild
Bird or beast she calls her child.

Busy in her handsome house
Known as Space, she falls a-drowse;
Yet, in seeming, works on dreaming,
While beneath her groping hands
Fiends make havoc in her bands.

How her hussif'ry succeeds
She unknows or she unheeds,
All things making for Death's taking!
—So the green-gowned faeries say
Living over Blackmoor way.

Come then, brethren, let us sing,
From the dawn till evening!—
For we know not that we go not
When the day's pale pinions fold
Where those be that sang of old.

THOMAS HARDY (1840–1928)

Song—the owl

1

When cats run home and light is come,
  And dew is cold upon the ground,
And the far-off stream is dumb,
  And the whirring sail goes round,
  And the whirring sail goes round;
    Alone and warming his five wits,
    The white owl in the belfry sits.

2

When merry milkmaids click the latch,
  And rarely smells the new-mown hay,
And the cock hath sung beneath the thatch
  Twice or thrice his roundelay,
  Twice or thrice his roundelay;
    Alone and warming his five wits,
    The white owl in the belfry sits.

ALFRED LORD TENNYSON (1809–1892)

Tawny owl *Thomas Bewick*

To a waterfowl

Whither, midst falling dew,
  While glow the heavens with the last steps of day,
Far, through their rosy depths, dost thou pursue
    Thy solitary way?

Vainly the fowler's eye
  Might mark thy distant flight to do thee wrong,
As, darkly seen against the crimson sky,
    Thy figure floats along.

Seek'st thou the plashy brink
Of weedy lake, or marge of river wide,
Or where the rocking billows rise and sink
    On the chafed ocean-side?

There is a Power whose care
Teaches thy way along that pathless coast—
The desert and illimitable air—
    Lone wandering, but not lost.

All day thy wings have fanned,
At that far height, the cold, thin atmosphere,
Yet stoop not, weary, to the welcome land,
    Though the dark night is near.

And soon that toil shall end;
Soon shalt thou find a summer home, and rest,
And scream among thy fellows; reeds shall bend,
    Soon, o'er thy sheltered nest.

Ducks *Carlo Crivelli*

38

Thou'rt gone, the abyss of heaven
Hath swallowed up thy form; yet, on my heart
Deeply has sunk the lesson thou hast given,
    And shall not soon depart.

He who, from zone to zone,
Guides through the boundless sky thy certain flight,
In the long way that I must tread alone,
    Will lead my steps aright.

WILLIAM CULLEN BRYANT (1794–1878)

The eagle
Fragment

He clasps the crag with hooked hands:
Close to the sun in lonely lands,
Ring'd with the azure world, he stands.

The wrinkled sea beneath him crawls;
He watches from his mountain walls,
And like a thunderbolt he falls.

ALFRED LORD TENNYSON (1809–1892)

Hawk *Vittore Pisanello*

'I watched a blackbird'

I watched a blackbird on a budding sycamore
One Easter Day, when sap was stirring twigs to the core;
   I saw his tongue, and crocus-coloured bill
   Parting and closing as he turned his trill;
   Then he flew down, seized on a stem of hay,
And upped to where his building scheme was under way,
As if so sure a nest were never shaped on spray.

THOMAS HARDY (1840–1928)

Starling *Thomas Bewick*

Thomas Bewick

The Natural size

& bright
e stump

On a peacock

I

Thou foolish Bird, of Feathers proud,
Whose Lustre yet thine Eyes ne're see:
The gazing Wonder of the Crowd,
Beauteous, not to thy self, but Me!
Thy Hellish Voice doth those affright,
Whose Eyes were charmed at thy sight.

II

Vainly thou think'st, those Eyes of thine
Were such as sleepy *Argus* lost;
When he was touch'd with rod Divine,
Who lat of Vigilance did boast.
Little at best they'll thee avail,
Not in thine *Head*, but in thy *Tayl*.

III

Wisemen do *forward* look to try
What will in *following* Moments come:
Backward thy useless Eyes do ly,
Nor do enquire of *future* doom.
'Nothing can remedy what's past;
Wisedom must guard the present cast.'

IV

Our Eyes are best employ'd at home,
Not when they are on others plac'd:
From thine but little good can come,
Which never on thy self are cast:
What can of such a Tool be made:
A Tayl *well-furnish'd*, but an empty Head.

THOMAS HEYRICK (1649–94)

Peacock *Domenico Ghirlandaio*

C FABRITIVS 1654

Proud songsters

The thrushes sing as the sun is going,
 And the finches whistle in ones and pairs,
And as it gets dark loud nightingales
  In bushes
Pipe, as they can when April wears,
 As if all Time were theirs.

These are brand-new birds of twelve-months' growing,
Which a year ago, or less than twain,
No finches were, nor nightingales,
  Nor thrushes,
But only particles of grain,
 And earth, and air, and rain.

THOMAS HARDY (1840–1928)

Goldfinch *Karel Fabritius*

To a skylark

Hail to thee, blithe spirit!
Bird thou never wert—
That from heaven or near it
Pourest thy full heart
In profuse strains of unpremeditated art.

Higher still and higher
From the earth thou springest,
Like a cloud of fire;
The blue deep thou wingest,
And singing still dost soar, and soaring ever singest.

In the golden light'ning
Of the sunken sun,
O'er which clouds are bright'ning,
Thou dost float and run,
Like an unbodied joy whose race is just begun.

The pale purple even
Melts around thy flight;
Like a star of heaven,
In the broad daylight
Thou art unseen, but yet I hear thy shrill delight—

Keen as are the arrows
Of that silver sphere
Whose intense lamp narrows
In the white dawn clear,
Until we hardly see, we feel that it is there.

All the earth and air
With thy voice is loud
As, when night is bare,
From one lonely cloud
The moon rains out her beams, and heaven is overflow'd.

What thou art we know not;
  What is most like thee?
From rainbow clouds there flow not
  Drops so bright to see,
As from thy presence showers a rain of melody:—

  Like a poet hidden
    In the light of thought,
  Singing hymns unbidden,
    Till the world is wrought
To sympathy with hopes and fears it heeded not:

  Like a high-born maiden
    In a palace tower,
  Soothing her love-laden
    Soul in secret hour
With music sweet as love, which overflows her bower:

  Like a glow-worm golden
    In a dell of dew,
  Scattering unbeholden
    Its aërial hue
Among the flowers and grass which screen it from the view:

  Like a rose embower'd
    In its own green leaves,
  By warm winds deflower'd,
    Till the scent it gives
Makes faint with too much sweet these heavy-wingèd thieves:

Sound of vernal showers
  On the twinkling grass,
Rain-awaken'd flowers—
  All that ever was
Joyous and clear and fresh—thy music doth surpass.

Teach us, sprite or bird,
  What sweet thoughts are thine:
I have never heard
  Praise of love or wine
That panted forth a flood of rapture so divine.

Chorus hymeneal,
  Or triumphal chant,
Match'd with thine would be all
  But an empty vaunt—
A thing wherein we feel there is some hidden want.

What objects are the fountains
  Of thy happy strain?
What fields, or waves, or mountains?
  What shapes of sky or plain?
What love of thine own kind? what ignorance of pain?

With thy clear keen joyance
  Languor cannot be:
Shadow of annoyance
  Never came near thee:
Thou lovest, but ne'er knew love's sad satiety.

Waking or asleep,
  Thou of death must deem
Things more true and deep
  Than we mortals dream,
Or how could thy notes flow in such a crystal stream?

We look before and after,
    And pine for what is not:
Our sincerest laughter
    With some pain is fraught;
Our sweetest songs are those that tell of saddest thought.

Yet, if we could scorn
    Hate and pride and fear,
If we were things born
    Not to shed a tear,
I know not how thy joy we ever should come near.

Better than all measures
    Of delightful sound,
Better than all treasures
    That in books are found,
Thy skill to poet were, thou scorner of the ground!

Teach me half the gladness
    That thy brain must know;
Such harmonious madness
    From my lips would flow,
The world should listen then, as I am listening now.

PERCY BYSSHE SHELLEY (1792–1822)

Goldfinch *Vittore Carpaccio*

The ousel-cock so black of hue

The ousel-cock, so black of hue,
   With orange-tawny bill,
The throstle with his note so true,
   The wren with little quill;
The finch, the sparrow, and the lark,
   The plain-song cuckoo gray,
Whose note full many a man doth mark,
   And dares not answer nay.

WILLIAM SHAKESPEARE (1564–1616)

King and Queen of the Pelicans *Edward Lear*

from:

The pelican chorus

King and Queen of the Pelicans we;
　No other birds so grand we see!
None but we have feet like fins!
With lovely leathery throats and chins!
Ploffskin, Pluffskin, Pelican jee!
We think no birds so happy as we!
Plumpskin, Ploshkin, Pelican jill!
We think so then, and we thought so still!

We live on the Nile. The Nile we love.
By night we sleep on the cliffs above.
By day we fish, and at eve we stand
On long bare islands of yellow sand.
And when the sun sinks slowly down
And the great rock walls grow dark and brown,
Where the purple river rolls fast and dim
And the ivory Ibis starlike skim,
Wing to wing we dance around,—
Stamping our feet with a flumpy sound,—
Opening our mouths as Pelicans ought,
And this is the song we nightly snort:

Ploffskin, Pluffskin, Pelican jee!
We think no Birds so happy as we!
Plumpskin, Ploshkin, Pelican jill!
We think so then, and we thought so still.

EDWARD LEAR (1812–1888)

The wild swans at Coole

The trees are in their autumn beauty,
The woodland paths are dry,
Under the October twilight the water
Mirrors a still sky;
Upon the brimming water among the stones
Are nine and fifty swans.

The nineteenth Autumn has come upon me
Since I first made my count;
I saw, before I had well finished,
All suddenly mount
And scatter wheeling in great broken rings
Upon their clamorous wings.

I have looked upon those brilliant creatures,
And now my heart is sore.
All's changed since I, hearing at twilight,
The first time on this shore,
The bell-beat of their wings above my head,
Trod with a lighter tread.

Unwearied still, lover by lover,
They paddle in the cold,
Companionable streams or climb the air;
Their hearts have not grown old;
Passion or conquest, wander where they will,
Attend upon them still.

But now they drift on the still water,
Mysterious, beautiful;
Among what rushes will they build,
By what lake's edge or pool
Delight men's eyes when I awake some day
To find they have flown away?

w. b. yeats (1865–1939)

Enraged swan *Jan Asselijn*

To the cuckoo

O blithe New-comer! I have heard,
I hear thee and rejoice.
O Cuckoo! shall I call thee Bird,
Or but a wandering Voice!

While I am lying on the grass
Thy twofold shout I hear,
From hill to hill it seems to pass,
At once far off, and near.

Though babbling only to the Vale,
Of sunshine and of flowers,
Thou bringest unto me a tale
Of visionary hours.

Thrice welcome, darling of the Spring!
Even yet thou art to me
No bird, but an invisible thing,
A voice, a mystery;

The same whom in my school-boy days
I listened to; that Cry
Which made me look a thousand ways
In bush, and tree, and sky.

To seek thee did I often rove
Through woods and on the green;
And thou wert still a hope, a love;
Still longed for, never seen.

Cuckoo *Thomas Bewick*

And I can listen to thee yet;
Can lie upon the plain
And listen, till I do beget
That golden time again.

O blessed Bird! the earth we pace
Again appears to be
An unsubstantial, faery place;
That is fit home for Thee!

WILLIAM WORDSWORTH (1770–1850)

Phyllyp Sparrowe

It was so prety a fole,
It wold syt on a stole,
And lerned after my scole
For to kepe his cut,
With, Phyllyp, kepe your cut!
   It had a veluet cap,
And wold syt vpon my lap,
And seke after small wormes,
And somtyme white bred crommes;
And many tymes and ofte
Betwene my brestes softe
It wolde lye and rest;
It was propre and prest.
   Somtyme he wolde gaspe
Whan he sawe a waspe;
A fly or a gnat,
He wolde flye at that;
And prytely he wold pant
Whan he saw an ant;
Lord, how he wolde pry
After the butterfly!
Lorde, how he wolde hop
After the gressop!
And whan I sayd, Phyp, Phyp,
Than he wold lepe and skyp,
And take me by the lyp.

Thomas Bewick

Alas, it wyll me slo,
That Phillyp is gone me fro!
Si in i qui ta tes,
Alas, I was euyll at ease!
De pro fun dis cla ma vi,
Whan I sawe my sparrowe dye!
   .   .   .   .   .
For it wold come and go,
And fly so to and fro;
And on me it wolde lepe
Whan I was aslepe,
And his fethers shake
Wherewith he wolde make
Me often for to wake,
And for to take him in
Vpon my naked skyn;
God wot, we thought no syn:
What though he crept so lowe?
It was no hurt, I trowe,
He dyd nothynge, perde,
But syt vpon my kne:
Phyllyp, though he were nyse,
In him it was no vyse;
Phyllyp had leue to go
To pyke my lytell too;
Phillip myght be bolde
And do what he wolde;
Phillip wolde seke and take
All the flees blake
That he coulde there espye
With his wanton eye.

JOHN SKELTON (1460–1529)

Town owl

On eves of cold, when slow coal fires,
rooted in basements, burn and branch,
brushing with smoke the city air;

When quartered moons pale in the sky,
and neons glow along the dark
like deadly nightshade on a briar;

Above the muffled traffic then
I hear the owl, and at his note
I shudder in my private chair.

For like an auger he has come
to roost among our crumbling walls,
his blooded talons sheathed in fur.

Some secret lure of time it seems
has called him from his country wastes
to hunt a newer wasteland here.

And where the candelabra swung,
bright with the dancers' thousand eyes,
now his black, hooded pupils stare,

And where the silk-shoed lovers ran
with dust of diamonds in their hair,
he opens now his silent wing,

And, like a stroke of doom, drops down,
and swoops across the empty hall,
and plucks a quick mouse off the stair . . .

LAURIE LEE (1914–)

Little owl *Albrecht Dürer*

508

To hear an oriole sing

To hear an oriole sing
May be a common thing,
Or only a divine.

It is not of the bird
Who sings the same, unheard,
As unto crowd

The fashion of the ear
Attireth that it hear
In dun or fair.

So whether it be rune,
Or whether it be none,
Is of within;

The 'tune is in the tree,'
The sceptic showeth me;
'No, sir! In thee!'

EMILY DICKINSON (1830–1886)

Baltimore Oriole *J. J. Audubon*

The jackdaw

There is a bird who, by his coat,
And by the hoarseness of his note,
   Might be suppos'd a crow;
A great frequenter of the church,
Where, bishop-like, he finds a perch,
   And dormitory too.

Above the steeple shines a plate,
That turns and turns, to indicate
   From what point blows the weather.
Look up—your brains begin to swim,
'Tis in the clouds—that pleases him,
   He chooses it the rather.

Fond of the speculative height,
Thither he wings his airy flight,
   And thence securely sees
The bustle and the raree-show
That occupy mankind below,
   Secure and at his ease.

You think, no doubt, he sits and muses
On future broken bones and bruises,
   If he should chance to fall.
No; not a single thought like that
Employs his philosophic pate,
   Or troubles it at all.

He sees, that this great roundabout—
The world, with all its motley rout,
   Church, army, physic, law,
Its customs, and its bus'nesses,—
Is no concern at all of his,
   And says—what says he?—Caw.

Thrice happy bird! I too have seen
Much of the vanities of men;
    And, sick of having seen 'em,
Would cheerfully these limbs resign
For such a pair of wings as thine,
    And such a head between 'em.

WILLIAM COWPER (1731–1800)

Jay *Giovanni da Udine*

Mocking bird *Mark Catesby*

The mocking-bird

from: Out of The Cradle Endlessly Rocking

Once, Paumanok,
When the snows had melted, and the Fifth-month grass was
      growing,
Up this sea-shore, in some briers,
Two guests from Alabama—two together,

And their nest, and four light-green eggs, spotted with brown,
And every day the he-bird, to and fro, near at hand,
And every day the she-bird, crouched on her nest, silent, with
      bright eyes,
And every day I, a curious boy, never too close, never
      disturbing them,
Cautiously peering, absorbing, translating.

Shine! shine! shine!
Pour down your warmth, great Sun!
While we bask—we two together.

Two together!
Winds blow south, or winds blow north,
Day come white, or night come black,
Home, or rivers and mountains from home,
Singing all time, minding no time,
If we two but keep together.

Till, of a sudden,
Maybe killed, unknown to her mate,
One forenoon the she-bird crouched not on the nest,
Nor returned that afternoon, nor the next,
Nor ever appeared again.

And thenceforward, all summer, in the sound of the sea,
And at night, under the full of the moon, in calmer weather,
Over the hoarse surging of the sea,

Or flitting from bier to brier by day,
I saw, I heard at intervals, the remaining one, the he-bird,
The solitary guest from Alabama.

Blow! blow! blow!
Blow up, sea-winds, along Paumanok's shore!
I wait and O wait, till you blow my mate to me.

Yes, when the stars glistened,
All night long, on the prong of a moss-scalloped stake,
Down, almost amid the slapping waves,
Sat the lone singer, wonderful, causing tears.

He called on his mate;
He poured forth the meanings which I, of all men, know.

WALT WHITMAN (1819–1892)

Robin *Thomas Bewick*

Robin Redbreast

Robin on a leafless bough,
    Lord in Heaven, how he sings!
Now cold Winter's cruel Wind
    Makes playmates of poor, dead things.

How he sings for joy this morn!
    How his breast doth pant and glow!
Look you how he stands and sings,
    Half-way up his legs in snow!

If these crumbs of bread were pearls,
    And I had no bread at home,
He should have them for that song;
    Pretty Robin Redbreast, Come.

W. H. DAVIES (1871–1940)

Ode to a nightingale

My heart aches, and a drowsy numbness pains
    My sense, as though of hemlock I had drunk,
Or emptied some dull opiate to the drains
    One minute past, and Lethe-wards had sunk:
'Tis not through envy of thy happy lot,
    But being too happy in thy happiness,
        That thou, light-wingèd Dryad of the trees,
            In some melodious plot
Of beechen green, and shadows numberless,
    Singest of summer in full-throated ease.

O for a draught of vintage! that hath been
    Cool'd a long age in the deep-delvèd earth,
Tasting of Flora and the country-green,
    Dance, and Provençal song, and sunburnt mirth!
O for a beaker full of the warm South!
    Full of the true, the blushful Hippocrene,
        With beaded bubbles winking at the brim,
            And purple-stainèd mouth;
That I might drink, and leave the world unseen,
    And with thee fade away into the forest dim:

Fade far away, dissolve, and quite forget
    What thou among the leaves hast never known,
The weariness, the fever, and the fret
    Here, where men sit and hear each other groan;
Where palsy shakes a few, sad, last grey hairs,
    Where youth grows pale, and spectre-thin, and dies;
        Where but to think is to be full of sorrow
            And leaden-eyed despairs;
    Where beauty cannot keep her lustrous eyes,
        Or new Love pine at them beyond to-morrow.

Away! away! for I will fly to thee,
  Not charioted by Bacchus and his pards,
But on the viewless wings of Poesy,
  Though the dull brain perplexes and retards:
Already with thee! tender is the night,
  And haply the Queen-Moon is on her throne,
    Cluster'd around by all her starry Fays;
      But here there is no light,
Save what from heaven is with the breezes blown
  Through verdurous glooms and winding mossy ways.

I cannot see what flowers are at my feet,
  Nor what soft incense hangs upon the boughs,
But, in embalmèd darkness, guess each sweet
  Wherewith the seasonable month endows
The grass, the thicket, and the fruit-tree wild;
  White hawthorn, and the pastoral eglantine;
    Fast-fading violets cover'd up in leaves;
      And mid-May's eldest child,
The coming musk-rose, full of dewy wine,
  The murmurous haunt of flies on summer eves.

Darkling I listen; and for many a time
  I have been half in love with easeful Death,
Call'd him soft names in many a musèd rhyme,
  To take into the air my quiet breath;
Now more than ever seems it rich to die,
  To cease upon the midnight with no pain,
    While thou art pouring forth thy soul abroad
      In such an ecstasy!
Still wouldst thou sing, and I have ears in vain—
  To thy high requiem become a sod.

Thou wast not born for death, immortal Bird!
No hungry generations tread thee down;
The voice I hear this passing night was heard
In ancient days by emperor and clown:
Perhaps the self-same song that found a path
Through the sad heart of Ruth, when, sick for home,
She stood in tears amid the alien corn;
The same that oftimes hath
Charm'd magic casements, opening on the foam
Of perilous seas, in faery lands forlorn.

Forlorn! the very word is like a bell
To toll me back from thee to my sole self!
Adieu! the fancy cannot cheat so well
As she is famed to do, deceiving elf.
Adieu! adieu! thy plaintive anthem fades
Past the near meadows, over the still stream,
Up the hill-side; and now 'tis buried deep
In the next valley-glades:
Was it a vision, or a waking dream?
Fled is that music:—do I wake or sleep?

JOHN KEATS (1795–1821)

The black vulture

Aloof upon the day's immeasured dome,
    He holds unshared the silence of the sky.
    Far down his bleak, relentless eyes descry
The eagle's empire and the falcon's home—
Far down, the galleons of sunset roam;
    His hazards on the sea of morning lie;
    Serene, he hears the broken tempest sigh
Where cold sierras gleam like scattered foam.

And least of all he holds the human swarm—
    Unwitting now that envious men prepare
    To make their dream and its fulfillment one,
When, poised above the caldrons of the storm,
    Their hearts, contemptuous of death, shall dare
    His roads between the thunder and the sun.

GEORGE STERLING (1869–1926)

Vulture *Irene Hawkins*

Seynt Valentynes Day

from: The Parliament of Fowls

Ther mighte men the royal egle finde,
That with his sharpe look perceth the sonne;
And other egles of a lower kinde,
Of which that clerkes wel devysen conne.
Ther was the tyraunt with his fethres donne
And greye, I mene the goshauk, that doth pyne
To briddes for his outrageous ravyne.

The gentil faucon, that with his feet distreyneth
The kinges hond; the hardy sperhauk eke,
The quayles foo; the merlion that peyneth
Him-self ful ofte, the larke for to seke;
Ther was the douve, with hir eyen meke;
The jalous swan, ayens his deth that singeth;
The oule eke, that of dethe the bode bringeth;

The crane the geaunt, with his trompes soune;
The thief, the chogh; and eke the jangling pye;
The scorning jay; the eles foo, the heroune;
The false lapwing, ful of treacherye;
The stare, that the counseyl can bewrye;
The tame ruddock, and the coward kyte;
The cok, that orloge is of thorpes lyte;

The sparow, Venus sone; the nightingale,
That clepeth forth the fresshe leves newe;
The swalow, mordrer of the flyes smale
That maken hony of floures fresshe of hewe;
The wedded turtel, with hir herte trewe;
The pecock, with his aungels fethres brighte;
The fesaunt, scorner of the cok by nighte;

Titmouse *Ellen Power*

72

The waker goos; the cukkow ever unkinde;
The papingay, ful of delicasye;
The drake, stroyer of his owne kinde;
The stork, the wreker of avouterye;
The hote cormeraunt of glotonye;
The raven wys, the crow with vois of care;
The throstel olde; the frosty feldefare.

What shulde I seyn? of foules every kinde
That in this worlde han fethres and stature,
Men mighten in that place assembled finde
Before the noble goddesse Nature.
And everich of hem did his besy cure
Benignely to chese or for to take,
By hir accord, his formel or his make.

GEOFFREY CHAUCER (1367–1434)

St Francis preaching to the birds *Giotto*

The birds

from: Milton, Book II

Thou hearest the Nightingale begin the Song of Spring:
The Lark, sitting upon his earthy bed, just as the morn
Appears, listens silent; then, springing from the waving
    cornfield, loud
He leads the Choir of Day—trill! trill! trill! trill!
Mounting upon the wings of light into the Great Expanse,
Re-echoing against the lovely blue and shining heavenly Shell;
His little throat labours with inspiration; every feather
On throat and breast and wings vibrates with the effluence
    Divine.
All Nature listens silent to him, and the awful Sun
Stands still upon the mountain looking on this little Bird
With eyes of soft humility and wonder, love and awe.
Then loud from their green covert all the Birds begin their
    song:
The Thrush, the Linnet and the Goldfinch, Robin and the
    Wren
Awake the Sun from his sweet revery upon the mountain:
The Nightingale again assays his song, and thro' the day
And thro' the night warbles luxuriant; every Bird of song
Attending his loud harmony with admiration and love.

WILLIAM BLAKE (1757–1827)

Cock *Thomas Bewick*

Chauntecleer

from: The Nonnes Preestes Tale

A yeerd she hadde, enclosed al aboute
With stikkes, and a drye dych withoute,
In which she hadde a cok, hight Chauntecleer.
In al the land, of crowyng nas his peer.
His voys was murier than the murie orgon
On messe-dayes that in the chirche gon.
Wel sikerer was his crowying in his logge
Than is a clokke or an abbey orlogge.
By nature he knew ech ascencioun
Of the equynoxial in thilke toun;
For whan degrees fiftene weren ascended,
Thanne crew he, that it myghte nat been amended.
His coomb was redder than the fyn coral,
And batailled as it were a castel wal;
His byle was blak, and as the jeet it shoon;
Lyk asure were his legges and his toon;
His nayles whitter than the lylye flour,
And lyk the burned gold was his colour.
This gentil cok hadde in his governaunce
Sevene hennes for to doon al his plesaunce,
Whiche were his sustres and his paramours,
And wonder lyk to hym, as of colours;
Of whiche the fairest hewed on hir throte
Was cleped faire damoysele Pertelote.
Curteys she was, discreet, and debonaire,
And compaignable, and bar hyrself so faire,
Syn thilke day that she was seven nyght oold,
That trewely she hath the herte in hoold
Of Chauntecleer, loken in every lith;
He loved hire so that wel was hym therwith.

GEOFFREY CHAUCER (1343–1400)

The Siskins

The bank swallows veer and dip,
Diving down at my windows,
Then flying almost straight upward,
Like bats in daytime,
And their shadows, bigger,
Race over the thick grass;
And the finches pitch through the air, twittering;
And the small mad siskins flit by,
Flying upward in little skips and erratic leaps;
Or they sit sideways on limber dandelion stems,
Bending them down to the ground;
Or perch and peck at larger flower-crowns,
Springing, one to another,
The last abandoned stalk always quivering
Back into straightness;
Or they fling themselves against tree trunks,
Scuttling down and around like young squirrels,
Birds furious as bees.

Now they move all together!—
These airy hippety-hop skippers,
Light as seed blowing off thistles!
And I seem to lean forward,
As my eyes follow after
Their sunlit leaping.

THEODORE ROETHKE (1908–1962).

Siskins J. J. Audubon

Little Trotty Wagtail

Little trotty wagtail he went in the rain,
And tittering, tottering sideways he ne'er got straight again,
He stooped to get a worm, and looked up to get a fly,
And then he flew away ere his feathers they were dry.

Little trotty wagtail, he waddled in the mud,
And left his little footmarks, trample where he would.
He waddled in the water-pudge, and waggle went his tail
And chirrupt up his wings to dry upon the garden rail.

Little trotty wagtail, you nimble all about,
And in the dimpling water-pudge you waddle in and out;
Your home is nigh at hand, and in the warm pig-stye,
So little Master Wagtail, I'll bid you a good-bye.

JOHN CLARE (1793–1864)

From an ancient Roman mosaic

Pigeon

A cropped, grey, too-small, bullet, Prussian head
Leading a body closely modelled on
A silly clay model for the sporting gun.

One shoos the other from the scattered bread,
Prolonging needlessly a marital
Irascibility. The bill could well

Support a pair of spectacles: instead,
All who will closely look at once espy
A geometrical and insane eye.

ROY FULLER (1912–   )

Pigeon *Thomas Bewick*

A bird came down the walk

A bird came down the walk:
He did not know I saw;
He bit an angle-worm in halves
And ate the fellow, raw.

And then he drank a dew
From a convenient grass,
And then hopped sidewise to the wall
To let a beetle pass.

He glanced with rapid eyes
That hurried all abroad,—
They looked like frightened beads, I thought
He stirred his velvet head

Like one in danger; cautious,
I offered him a crumb,
And he unrolled his feathers
And rowed him softer home

Than oars divide the ocean,
Too silver for a seam,
Or butterflies, off banks of noon,
Leap, plashless, as they swim.

EMILY DICKINSON (1830–1886)

Heron *Fifteenth-century tapestry*

Hawk roosting

I sit in the top of the wood, my eyes closed.
Inaction, no falsifying dream
Between my hooked head and hooked feet:
Or in sleep rehearse perfect kills and eat.

The convenience of the high trees!
The air's buoyancy and the sun's ray
Are of advantage to me;
And the earth's face upward for my inspection.

My feet are locked upon the rough bark.
It took the whole of Creation
To produce my foot, my each feather:
Now I hold Creation in my foot

Or fly up, and revolve it all slowly—
I kill where I please because it is all mine.
There is no sophistry in my body:
My manners are tearing off heads—

The allotment of death.
For the one path of my flight is direct
Through the bones of the living.
No arguments assert my right:

The sun is behind me.
Nothing has changed since I began.
My eye has permitted no change.
I am going to keep things like this.

TED HUGHES (1930–   )

To a marsh hawk in Spring

There is health in thy gray wing,
Health of nature's furnishing.
Say, thou modern-winged antique,
Was thy mistress ever sick?
In each having of thy wing
Thou dost health and leisure bring,
Thou dost waive disease and pain
And resume new life again.

HENRY DAVID THOREAU (1817–1862)

Hawk *J. B. Oudry*

'O nightingale . . .'

O nightingale, that on yon bloomy Spray
    Warbl'st at eeve, when all the Woods are still,
    Thou with fresh hope the Lovers heart dost fill,
    While the jolly hours lead on propitious *May*,
Thy liquid notes that close the eye of Day,
    First heard before the shallow Cuccoo's bill
    Portend success in love; O if *Jove's* will
    Have linkt that amorous power to thy soft lay,
Now timely sing, ere the rude Bird of Hate
    Foretell my hopeless doom in som Grove ny:
    As thou from year to year hast sung too late
For my relief; yet hadst no reason why,
    Whether the Muse, or Love call thee his mate,
    Both them I serve, and of their train am I.

JOHN MILTON (1608–1674)

A minor bird

I have wished a bird would fly away,
And not sing by my house all day;

Have clapped my hands at him from the door
When it seemed as if I could bear no more.

The fault must partly have been in me.
The bird was not to blame for his key.

And of course there must be something wrong
In wanting to silence any song.

ROBERT FROST (1875–1963)

Nightingale *Thomas Bewick*

Acknowledgments

The editor and publishers would like to thank the following for permission to reproduce certain copyright poems:

W. H. Davies, *Robin Redbreast*, from THE COMPLETE POEMS OF W. H. DAVIES: Mrs H. M. Davies, copyright 1963, Jonathan Cape Limited, London and Wesleyan University Press, Middletown, Connecticut.

Robert Frost, *A Minor Bird*: the Estate of Robert Frost and Edward Connery Latham, editor of THE POETRY OF ROBERT FROST (Jonathan Cape Limited, London and Holt, Rinehart and Winston, Inc., New York).

Roy Fuller, *Pigeon*: André Deutsch and Curtis Brown Limited, London.

Thomas Hardy, *The Bullfinches, Proud Songsters* and *I watched a blackbird*, from THE COLLECTED POEMS: The Trustees of the Hardy Estate and Macmillan, London and Basingstoke, and Macmillan Publishing Company, New York.

Ralph Hodgson, *The sedge-warbler*: Mrs Hodgson and Macmillan, London and Basingstoke, and St Martin's Press, Inc., Macmillan & Company Limited, New York.

Ted Hughes, *Hawk Roosting*, from LUPERCAL, copyright 1959 by Ted Hughes. Reprinted by permission of Faber and Faber Limited, London, and Harper and Row Publishers Inc., New York.

Laurie Lee, *Town Owl*: André Deutsch, London.

Walter de la Mare, *A Robin* (from THE COLLECTED POEMS OF WALTER DE LA MARE): The Literary Trustees of Walter de la Mare, and the Society of Authors as their representative.

Theodore Roethke, *The Siskins*, copyright 1953 by Theodore Roethke (from THE COLLECTED POEMS OF THEODORE ROETHKE). Reprinted by permission of Faber and Faber Limited, London, and Doubleday and Company, Inc., New York.

George Sterling, *The black vulture*: A. M. Robertson Publishing Company, San Francisco.

W. B. Years, *The wild swans at Coole*, (from THE COLLECTED POEMS OF W. B. YEATS): by permission of M. B. Yeats and the Macmillan Company of London and Basingstoke, and Macmillan Publishing Company, Inc., New York.

While the editor and publishers have made every effort to obtain permission from the copyright holders of the poems and illustrations in this book, they would be most grateful to learn of any instances where an incomplete or incorrect acknowledgment has been made.